T0120659

STRIKE ONE; YOU'RE OUT

Frederick Smith

authorHOUSE®

AuthorHouse™
1663 Liberty Drive
Bloomington, IN 47403
www.authorhouse.com
Phone: 833-262-8899

© 2021 Frederick Smith. All rights reserved.

No part of this book may be reproduced, stored in a retrieval system, or transmitted by any means without the written permission of the author.

Published by AuthorHouse 03/26/2021

ISBN: 978-1-6655-2131-4 (sc)
ISBN: 978-1-6655-2134-5 (e)

Print information available on the last page.

Any people depicted in stock imagery provided by Getty Images are models, and such images are being used for illustrative purposes only. Certain stock imagery © Getty Images.

All scriptures were taken from the King James Version Bible.

This book is printed on acid-free paper.

Because of the dynamic nature of the Internet, any web addresses or links contained in this book may have changed since publication and may no longer be valid. The views expressed in this work are solely those of the author and do not necessarily reflect the views of the publisher, and the publisher hereby disclaims any responsibility for them.

Contents

INTRODUCTION

My last 2 books I knew were super important for Christians. I thought I was done and would just Preach the rest when God gave the audience. Then this subject just kept burning in my spirit that must be brought to light even though it's in my 2 previous books. I've found that most don't seem to understand the debt of scriptures in revelation even though I am not educated and use layman's wording. So I'm bringing this subject out separate and in more detail.

I said before about the "3 Strikes you're OUT" meaning in Revelation 14:9-11. It says WHO only of humans will be tormented forever in the Lake of Fire, because all sinners will NOT be like we have been told all our lives by Churches. It says; "…if any man worship the Beast and his Image and receives his MARK shall be tormented day and night forever with no rest". That is plain and needs no interpretation. 3 things a human has to do to get the same forever torment as the devil and his angels. If sinner humans don't do ALL 3 of these they will go to the Lake of Fire, but will eventually die out by the second death after they have paid for ALL their sins. Rev. 21:8 "…shall have THEIR part in the Lake.." & "Every idle word shall be brought into Judgment" Jesus said.

But what about this Title of ONE Strike You're OUT? Out of what? This book gives all the scripture details of this but I will let you in on the super points in this introduction. This comes from Revelation 13:8; "…ALL that dwell on the face of the earth shall worship him whose names are NOT written in the LAMBS book of Life…" All here means even MOST baptized Christian believers will worship [think highly of] this beast. Yes they will be fooled at this stage but for different reasons. This book will show the reasons they will WANT to believe him. Please remember that this praise of the first beast comes a year or more before the 2nd beast and devil get BACK to this earth. These fooled ones will only see their mistake when the 2nd beast comes in and demand they ALSO worship the Image AND get the MARK. Then they will regret their mistake because that FIRST strike will cause them to MISS heaven PERIOD. NO forgiveness for that at all.

I'm going to show just 3 Revelation scriptures now and the rest you will read in the book. Revelation 15:2 & 20:4 & 21:27. 15:2 & 20:4 both say "… they got the victory over the Beast 1; Image 2; & Mark 3. They did not fall for even 1 of the devils tricks. Notice also these are On the Sea of Glass [Heaven] and part of the 1st Resurrection. These were NOT CAST back and out or told to depart like many JESUS said He would reject of Christians. Revelation 21:27 shows those who ONLY are in the Holy City of gold; Heaven on Earth that only Spirit beings can enter. It sits on the New Earth where those Christians who were FOOLED will be in another body of flesh not pure spirit. They must come up to that City once a year but can NOT go IN.

This book will cover all this in more detail for those truly interested in pleasing God and making heaven. Most Christians too lazy to check the scriptures. So they just believe whatever their denominational church teaches. Too many scriptures BORE todays Christians. Remember Jesus SPIT out Most in Revelation 3:16. He didn't say they weren't SAVED just they were LUKEWARM, [casual, mediocre, & average]. We have the power to not even fall for ONE trick of satan!

HOW THIS BOOK IS WRITTEN

This book is written basically for Christians. The unsaved will not know these scriptures and stories I refer to. But even they can see them, and get curious enough to accept Christ. There are scriptures especially in Revelation that even Christians have never heard before. Ask yourself why you were never taught these things in church? Christians must start a personal and serious Bible study on their own. The Lord will guide if you will use what He shows you for His work. He doesn't waste knowledge on people who will not use it. "Cast not thy pearls among the swine".

I get right to the points and don't waste time and words making this book longer. If a person is really concerned about their salvation they will go to the Bible and check these serious things I'm writing. Most will just ignore and keep depending on their churches to get them to Heaven.

I write mostly partial scriptures and show mostly where they are written so you can go check. If you don't you're not interested anyway. I seriously say Christians should know most of these scriptures and stories. Some are the Parables Jesus spoke, and churches gave the wrong or partial interpretations. I do know the Revelation scriptures you will have some trouble with. Don't let that worry you. Even I had read Revelation many years and NOT understood it. Then about 15 years ago the Spirit told me to go back and read about the 7 churches. I told the Lord "Lord I read that and didn't understand it". He spoke back and said "Read it backwards". Sound odd to you? Well it did to me also, but I did it. Low and behold I saw it. I read Laodicea about the casting out, then the 6th church Philadelphia and realized it was the Rapture by it saying "I have set before you and open door". And "I will keep you from the hour of temptation". So now I had a fix point. Everything before that must be what happens leading up to the Rapture. Then I saw the Rapture mentioned 6 other times in Rev. It took 10 more years before I had confidence to write the book "They Have Revelation Absolutely Wrong". If you want more details on Rev. you can get that.

This book is written in simple language and wording because my education level is very low. No college words because I never got even to high school. God doesn't need a scholar He needs willing hearts.

I pray this book either out of conviction, interest or fear, makes you really get into the Bible. Then re-think seriously what you have been taught while we still have time. "If the blind lead the blind BOTH fall into the ditch". My punishment [and all Teachers] will be much worse if I, or they mislead you. We go to the Lake of Fire.

CHAPTER 1
"Why they love the Beast [devil]"

N o one in his right mind would love the devil. So why do as the scripture says; "ALL worship him"? First we must know that the Bible is mostly for Christians because the unsaved "cannot please God nor understand" Romans 8:8. Any person can accept Christ and be given understanding of the Bible. So when Rev. 13:8 says ALL shall worship the hidden meaning is EVEN Christians. Proof is in the verse, it says "..Whose names are NOT written in the LAMBS book of Life". Jesus hinted in Rev. 3:5 He will blot OUT some [most] names out of HIS book. So why will even Christians prefer this horrible person.

Let's understand that chapters 11-13 are basically going on in the same time period. Before the 1ˢᵗ Beast gets here the 2 Witnesses and 144,000 have been here preaching the real truth exposing ALL false preaching by the denominational churches. Matthew 24:14 Jesus said before the end "THIS Gospel will be preached.". Not the watered down, miss interpreted, compromised Gospel that's made Christians so at ease about going to Heaven. Let's look at Rev. 13:3; "..one of his heads were wounded to death..". Now who is able on earth to SMITE such a powerful person who controls the armies and even has the devil's knowledge? But he does NOT die and that is a super miracle. WHY? Because he should have died. WHY?

Because the only person on earth at this time who can and will smite him is the 2 Witnesses. As I said before chapters 11-13 are going on about the same time. Chapter 11 tells the details of the 2

Witnesses and what they do. 11:5 says; ".. if anyone will hurt them fire comes out and devours [kills] them and they MUST in this manner be killed". These 2 get here before the 1st beast comes in. These 2 by this time have killed MANY but their words not literal fire and NO one ever survived it. Now this Beast gets smitten and lives. How and why? Because the 2 Witnesses time is up by then. He has done his job of exposing false doctrine for the Christians who will accept the REAL Gospel, and strengthened the church for when the 2nd Beast and get here later. [Rev. 12:6 for any who can understand it].

Once it's clear he didn't die he goes on a rampage and makes war with the REAL Christians, NOT the fake Christians Rev. 13:7. We must understand that there are 2 Churches in Rev. mentioned as WOMEN. Rev. 12:1 the real church and Rev. 17:1-7. 17:6 says "..she is drunken with blood of the [real] SAINTS..". Proving she's the fake church. Christian's greatest enemy is not the unsaved but the fake Christians. The bibles history shows the religious leaders killing the real prophets of God even Jesus Himself. The parable of the Wheat and Tares shows the tares got into Jesus property. Paul said satan's demons are transformed into angels of light and ministers of the gospel. These super rich Pastors today will KILL you about their money. Isaiah 66:5 tells of this also.

So let's get back to why they will love the Beast [devil}. The 2 Witnesses came and condemned the false and casual teachings of today's churches. They went against the rich mega pastors and all the denominations. The 144,000 helpers also go against them Rev. 2:2. So not only are the fake Christians mad at the 2 Witnesses the unsaved never wanted to hear all that either. They are comfortable in their sin and don't want anyone spoiling their fun. And the fake Christians are comfortable in their belief that God will forgive them for their lukewarm; half stepping; casual Christianity & some pure outright SIN. Churches have made a place for every kind of evil. There are churches ok with fornicators, racist, homosexuals, money lovers etc. Some condemn one sin but allow a worse one in theirs. But theses 2 Witnesses condemn them ALL.

Let's look at what these 2 are commanded to do by God. Rev. 11:1-3 John [one of the 2 Witnesses] is told "measure the temple and the alter and them that dwell there IN.". And leave out the courtyard of the temple where other believers are. In other words show who is accepted & ready for Heaven and TELL them so on earth. It is NOT a broad spectrum of Christians going to heaven. Jesus said "..Narrow and straight is the way'. Meaning hard and difficult. Those on the broad way go into hell. Matthew 7:13-14. **I must add something here about it being hard. Jesus also said His "yoke is easy and His burdens light". The only way it's hard is those who won't accept it ALL and try to have it both ways. To All who forsake all it is EASY not hard.**

Now the 2 Witnesses are told to Preach these hard facts and the world will HATE these 2 so much they would rather side with the DEVIL [beast]. Their comfort zone has been disturbed. They want it to be easy to get in heaven. They don't want to study the Bible but just let the Pastors tell them. They want to keep certain sins. Their hatred is so strong after the Beast KILLS these 2 in Rev. 11:7 which is Rev. 13:8 look what it says the world and FAKE Christians do Rev. 11:10. "They rejoice and send gifts one to another...[make a 2nd Christmas]...because these 2 Prophets TORMENTED them that dwell upon the earth". They hated what GOD said by these 2. God said in the Old Testament several times; "they haven't rejected you they rejected ME". Jesus said if you "reject Him you rejected the one who sent Him". So who are these people who say Preachers should Preach NICE? I have been told many times I'm too harsh and I judge people. I never judge. If I use Gods words it's not my judgment but HIS.

Isaiah 5:1-7 tells a story pf God making a Vineyard and does everything for it to produce the best. When harvest came it produced "WILD Grapes [grapes like any other place would produce]. God said; "what more could I have done.... And you decide what more could I have done". This referred to the way the JEWS acted after all He had done for them. Now look at the New Covenant under Jesus Christ. Look what kind of Christians we see today. They are

3

just like the unsaved. They lie, steal, fornicate, cuss, race HATE, homo, lovers of money etc. What more could Jesus have done for the Church. Truth is nothing more could have been done. We cannot blame Him even though many will try like Adam did in the Garden when he blamed God for giving him EVE who made him eat the forbidden fruit.

So in concluding this the main points are it's not that they LOVE the beast, but that they HATE the 2 Witnesses so strongly. Meaning they HATE God's requirements for Heaven. Christians are wishing their pastors are right and NOT the 2 Witnesses. They will gamble their eternal life on it and greatly regret it. These words have been in this same Bible all Churches use. Why didn't they tell you this? There is much more on the 1 Strike you're out in this book. Just start making your final decision now so you can build your Spiritual strength up to withstand what's coming.

It's not they love the Beast. It's they HATE Gods 2 Witnesses!!!!

CHAPTER 2
"Impossible to Fool Real Christians"

It's the Bible that says it's impossible to Fool Real Christians. Let me give you one of those scriptures now. John 6:39 "….. of all that HE has given Me I will lose NONE..". Jesus is showing a difference between the ones the Father sends Him and those who come for some other reason. The Father sees the hearts and knows those who are dead serious and of a "broken and contrite spirit" Psalms 51:17 God will not despise [turn away]. Many come to Christ with attitude and demands of their own that will not work. Jesus did say just Believe and be baptized and you will not Perish or be Condemned. Perish and Condemn means the Lake of Fire where no one ever comes back from. So He accepts those in His safety zone and hopes as they go to church and read the Bible they will eventually surrender all and be as the ones the Father sent. Or they will be cast out at the Rapture Judgment Seat of Christ at the 1st Resurrection to hell. At the 2nd Resurrection they can get the New Earth but not Heaven. All this is in detail in my Revelation book. There will be clearer scriptures on not being fooled later in this chapter.

First know the difference between a weakness of a sin and total belief of a false teaching. We all can have a weakness and sin. But we are so sorry for it we immediately repent and don't continue in it. "Sin shall not have dominance over us". This chapter talks of believers following false teachings continually in these denominational churches. The Holy Spirit has only one truth to tell. He doesn't tell one church one thing and another church another thing. Someone is mistaken or outright lying. We will examine some of these teachings from back then and NOW!

Galatians 3:1 "Oh foolish Galatians who has bewitched you.". 3:3 "..how could you have begun in the Spirit and now turned…". False Preachers can come along any and all the time and trick most believers. Paul had taught them well when he was there, but when he left scammers came in. False Preachers came along EVERY time Paul left a place to trick the people. Acts 20:29 Paul says about the Roman Church; "..I know that upon my departing grievous wolves SHALL come in not sparing the flock". Paul also said "of your own selves [Pastors] shall men arise to draw away people after themselves [not Christ]. Yes even your Pastors can turn on you and God. They can fall for the same lusts that tempt us all. Money is the main culprit along with sex. One thing you should notice is Paul was an Apostle and NO one can get false teaching by one of them.

The church at Corinth got into a problem with TONGUES. Thinking if you didn't speak in tongues you weren't really saved like some churches say today. They ignored all the other gifts of the Spirit and said tongues was the real Proof only. Both sides of my own family believe in tongues. I have been extremely pressured to get tongues by many. But I have NEVER spoken in tongues and now can teach all the scriptures on their mistake about them. But so many were fooled and pressured to the point of even faking tongues to get along in those churches. They will turn on you like they turned on Jesus about not going along with the crowd. This is in all denominational churches. Don't make waves; do as we do or get out. Remember what they put the man born blind through after Jesus healed him. Pressured him say it was not Jesus who did it.

When it comes to Christianity the majority does NOT rule. Jesus said many times FEW find life and LITTLE flock. Jesus said real Christians will be put OUT the churches. If you haven't been put out a church or 3 you may have compromised into a false doctrine. I've been run out of 9-10 I lost track. There are so many stories of Gods Prophets having to stand ALONE & die alone. Jesus said MANY will say to Him at Judgment "Lord we did this and that…& He will answer I never knew you". Great was the fall of that house. Feelings were crushed right at the supposed pay day of Heaven. Who wouldn't double check their beliefs while there's still time?

So what makes Christians fall for false teachings? James gives us 1 answer James 1:14 "..when he is drawn away of his OWN lusts". When don't want to follow ALL of Jesus teachings we look for and find a church that will ok what we don't want to change. Timothy says "they will heap to themselves teachers having itchy ears.". Pastors just saying what the people want and not what God says to tell them. This keeps the offering plates fuller and the seats. So it's not all the Pastors fault. There are churches for Racist, homosexuals, fornicators, etc. Those Real Christians who cannot be fooled made up their mind from day one they would forsake ALL for Jesus and the Father saw them and sent them to Jesus. Jesus can tell those the Father sent and those who came for other reasons. In John 6 where that verse is it happened after Jesus had feed the thousands. They came a long way to find Jesus the next day. Jesus told them you didn't come for ME but for more free food. Some want God when their broke or girlfriends leave or in jail or sick etc. Why did you come? There's a test coming that will prove if you are serious about Jesus or came for some other reason. Our money property and our very lives will be on the line.

Many are fooled because of the Human education these Pastors have today. Today you must have a human degree to Pastor a church. Human schools cannot teach Spiritual insights. But they fool most people. Paul was full of education but God had to send him away for 3 years to RE train him and get all that Junk he had learned from humans out of him. He said in Galatians 1:11-12 '...I neither received it from men NOR was I taught it......... but by revelation of Jesus Christ". You can't put new wine in old bottles. If you're full of knowledge how can God get His knowledge in you?

Now let's get to the undisputed scriptures on Real Christians NOT being fooled. Matthew 24:24 "..Many false Prophets will come and show GREAT signs....that **IF IT WAS POSSIBLE** would fool the very ELECT". It's not possible. And this is speaking of the last days and the 2ⁿᵈ beast that seems to give life to a statue. Just think of the billions of Christian's falling for these amateur fake preacher's today. They don't stand a chance when the devils top dog comes in.

John 10: 5 &27 Jesus says "My sheep hear My Voice [period]". Verse 5 says "…Strangers they will NOT follow [at all] for they don't know the voice of strangers". That needs no interpretation. It is absolute. Daniel 11:32-35 speaks of the end times also about the 144,000 helpers of the 2 Witnesses. "They that do know their GOD will take action.". Yes even with the death sentence for preaching over their heads they will do Christ's work. Is Jesus really #1 in your life? Or is He just a part? I wrote a study titled "A Side order of Christ". To most Jesus is not the main course.

John7:17 says; "..he that will DO the will of the Father SHALL know of the doctrine". God doesn't give out this info for you go uuh and ahh. If you won't get out there and boldly spread it it will not be given to you. We are all invited to Heaven. The New Earth is for those lukewarm and cowards. Those who let the Pastor do the research and study for them. If they study for you, you are almost certain to be fooled by false preachers.

CHAPTER 3
"Boldness & Death"

One of the main reasons Christians will fall for the 1st Strike is FEAR. When the 1st beast starts a War with the Saints [Rev. 13:7] fear will set in on most of the non-fully committed Christians. And I repeat again this war will be against the True Church revived by the 2 Witnesses and 144,000. The false churches will not be the target of the beast. Plus the 2nd beast; the False Prophet isn't even here yet to run those churches. They are being run by the organizing of the false churches leaders against the True Church. So in order to not be troubled by the wrath of the beast they will also side with him. You must understand this about the 2 Churches. One is big and wrong, the other is small and right. Rev. 2:9 speaks of this "...I know thy **poverty** [small in number]...and blasphemy of them who say they are Jews [Christians] and are NOT but are the church of satan". Never listen to people saying we all worship the same God and will be accepted in. Jesus was casting out false Christians all those times He said Depart; go; never knew you etc. ONLY Christians go to Christ's judgment at the 1st resurrection.

Let's look at several scriptures in Rev. first about accepting death if it comes to us because the false churches say we will have NO tribulation. Revelation 2:10 "...be faithful unto death and I will give you a crown of life". Plus it says "we SHALL have a tribulation". Rev. 6:9-11 "...I saw the souls of them SLAIN for the Word & testimony which they HELD [onto]". Rev. 12:11 "...they loved not their lives unto the death..". Ask ourselves the common question; why would the Saints of old have to go through those persecutions and trials and we NOT have too also? Why are we better than they? They didn't want it either but they accepted it for Heaven. They understood from the real Bible teachings that death was very possible. Today they tell us we will have it easy and no Tribulation. Rev. 20:4 tells of those "beheaded". Why does it only mention those that paid the ultimate price IN Heaven? Just to give us an example because the majority will not be killed, but the fear and scare when the killing starts will run most Christians away.

The seed on stony ground in Matthew 13 says with "...JOY they received the Word but when persecution and tribulation came they fell away". Why? Because they were not preached to about this part. So when it came they were surprised and say "I didn't sign up for this". Yes we all signed up for this even if your Pastors didn't tell you God's Bible told you. If you cared to check it. More about this as one of the 2 MAIN traps Jesus said would derail most. Remember He said we MUST "endure to the end". Most won't die but IF it comes we must accept it. Death is the devils last card to play to scare us from Christ and Heaven. The other is all our money and material things will be taken. Many will drop out then. Because their money always meant more than Jesus and they didn't realize it till it came.

Revelation 14:6 is the last Gospel to be preached on earth by the 2 Witnesses and starts with "Fear GOD". Why because most will fear the beast. That's why the Bible describes the beast in such a horrible way; 7 heads 10 horns, like leopard, lion, bear. And Daniel says "dreadful, terrible, devours, breaks in pieces, stumps residue under his feet! God wants to prepare for the worst so we will have strength to spare. Remember we are "MORE than conquerors". In competition people over train just in case they need it, but usually they don't. Scripture says "when the enemy comes in like a FLOOD". That so called flood is just a trickle to Christians who stay prayed up. I haven't seen floods only trickles so far. Most will be caught off guard & unprepared. Our strength comes from the Word. The more we study it and DO it the stronger we get. If too many scriptures bore you something is wrong? The spirit in us needs spiritual FOOD but most are starving the Spirit in them to death. We can be rich spiritually but poor materially.

Hebrews 11 tells of long list of saints throughout history who have stood up to unspeakable things for God. It says "…the world was not worthy," [to even have these Godly people down here]. But let's look at a few others like John the Baptist who knew if he told the king he was wrong to have his brother's wife he would be Killed. But he told him and died. Stephen who knew if he spoke that harsh to the Pharisees and blamed them for killing Jesus he would be killed. But he told them. They were saying let's get our death over with and out the way. They did not love their lives unto the death. I often say when they start back chopping of heads I will raise my hand and say "Me first". God help me to fulfill that saying and get it out the way. Jesus warned many times about who to fear for real. "Fear not them who kill the body and then has no more power…..fear Him who after he has killed has power to cast into hell". Imagine the terror of those who do horrible crimes then commit suicide thinking it's over. They wake up in the spirit world where GOD is in charge and there's no escape. They can't die from there until He allows it. They can be tormented worse than the harm they did to others on earth.

Remember the 3 Hebrew boys who wouldn't bow down to the king's statue in Daniel 3? Well he gave them 1 more chance to change their mind because he liked those 3. Their answer to the KING should be our answer today with same boldness Daniel 3:16 "..we are NOT careful to answer you in this matter….we will NOT bow down…..our God is able to deliver us…but if He doesn't we STILL won't bow down". They had made up their mind LONG before as every Christian does but doesn't realize we made up our minds also, supposedly to accept death if it comes. They were delivered and we know the story about how the king looked in the furnace and saw 4 not 3 in the fire and UN harmed.

There are many stories of boldness unto death but I'm only showing the ones I see as strongest for this book's title. Luke 14:26; 28; 33-35 Jesus says about being HIS disciple "…forsake even his own LIFE…" ….count the cost [before you accept ME] ..to see if you can [finish]". "…forsake ALL that you have..[money family etc.]…you can NOT be HIS..". When Jesus say be His he's saying ONLY those who are His will go to Heaven period. Rev. 21:27 about Heaven; "…only those written in the LAMBS book of life". Rev. 3:5 He will "BLOT most names Out of His book". "ye are the salt….if salt lose its savor it's good for NOTHING and is cast out". This is showing Jesus casting back many at His Judgment Seat in the 1st Resurrection. Why don't Pastors tell the whole truth when people come up to be saved. I tell people the "the devil just declared war on you".

The devil already has the unsaved sinners in his back pocket. He doesn't need to bother them. But when a person switches sides to Jesus you become his enemy. We were all born in sin belonging to the devil. When we are saved by accepting Christ we become alive. "Let the dead bury the dead". Jesus said meaning all that don't accept Him are dead already and going to the Lake of Fire. These scriptures should be kindergarten to people saved for years. But they don't study the Bible and don't think they need to. When we read and study we "eat Jesus flesh and drink His Blood" John 6. He said the Words He speaks are Spirit and life. Let's consume His Words.

Paul says in Hebrews 5 "..When we ought to be teachers we still have need to be taught" [even the basics of scripture]. Without BOLDNESS even to death [if it comes to us] we will try to get out of trouble by thinking the beast is a good guy to keep our lives easier. That 1 strike will cause us MISS out on Heaven. "He that will seek to save his life SHALL lose it" absolutely! Let's train and over train. We don't know how much pressure we will be put under yet. We should not get over confident in ourselves. My real dependence is to call on HIS power to make me accept death as He did. We are "More than conquerors through Christ who strengthens us". He is there to do what we can't do. When we did all we can He will carry us the rest of the way. "Be of good cheer, "I" have overcome the world'. Since he did it He will do it for us also.

CHAPTER 4
"Most Fooled Today by Amateurs"

The number one false prophet in Revelation hasn't even come yet and the Bible warns about his very convincing miracles. Jesus spoke of him and 2 Thess. Speaks of him also. Jesus said many times "MANY false prophets would come and deceive many [most]". Yes there have been fakes all through history and we will focus on a few scriptures and what we see is happening today. We see mega churches believing different doctrines and know the Holy Spirit only teaches ONE doctrine. So one or all are wrong period. Jesus said My sheep hear My voice. Just seeing over 100 different denominations proves some or ALL are not hearing Jesus voice. The New Testament church was on one accord.

2 Timothy 4:3-4 "..Time will come they will not endure sound [true] doctrine but heap to themselves after their own lusts teachers having itchy ears.." Whatever the people want to hear in the churches that is what the Pastors will preach OR avoid depending on the crowd. "And turn from truth unto fables [lies]". What kind of things will they want to hear? 2 Timothy 3:1-5 it gives a number of horrible personality traits that CHRISTIANS will have. When we read them we don't even think they are Christians. But the proof is in verse 5; "..Having a FORM of Godliness" [they go to church]. And it says "From such turn away". Yet people flock to these in great numbers. If they don't want to hear about hell they go to another church that never mentions hell. And the list goes on for sexual sins and racism. The Jews hated the Samaritan's with a passion and didn't care what

Jesus said about it or who His Father was. They hated them. Today we have race haters IN the churches. Even other sins that they demand must be right.

Paul said people would turn about to every wind of doctrine. Today people choose a church by many things except the right thing. Some for music, beauty of the building, looks of the Pastor, education level of the Pastor etc. Some because the teaching sounds good and humanly right to them. What about if it's wrong to God? He said "My thoughts are not your thoughts and your ways not My ways". "Lean not in our own understanding". This is what is called **self-righteousness! We decided what God should accept.** And many will go to Judgment to try and convince Jesus to accept it. Like in Matthew 7:22-23 "Lord we did miracles and wonderful works in your name". He tells them I never knew you". No explanation for you period. Check your works now because at Judgment there will be NO discussion. By being wrong on these things TODAY shows we are very likely to fall for beast and 1st strike.

1 Timothy 6:1-8 tells of Churches teaching prosperity doctrine that "Gain is Godliness". It says "Turn away from them". Yet these are the mega churches they flock TO not from them. Today's Christians are falling for amateurs. We see fake miracles all the time but no wheel chairs and crutches left behind. Yes God can heal but He hasn't given that power to anyone since the 1st century to have continually like back then. Imagine if a person really had that power to heal all manner of sickness? He would be swarmed and on every news in the world. Those gifts are gone **now.** We don't need them now we would abuse them now and sell their use now. 1 Corinthians 13 Paul says LOVE is all we need now. if you believe these people now you will fall for beast and get your strike 1.

Yes it is a little difficult for most to figure out so many things about the churches. But have you tried going back to square one and what you promised God at salvation? Did you really surrender all? Do you still have goals in this life? What comes before your duty to Jesus? 2 Corin. 5:15 about real Christians "..They live NOT for themselves". Do you live for yourself and monetary gain & family?

God can't use a person who already has an agenda. Yes we must work a job to pay bills and survive, but what about our free time? Do we have any free time for HIM? Watching sports is year around at 3 hours plus per game. What does that leave Him. It's nothing wrong with sports it's something wrong if we have no time work His work. Jesus said "Pray the Lord of the harvest send LABORORS into the vineyard". Workers are desperately needed.

When Pastors say it's done when we got saved they are wrong. Salvation part is done so we can start the WORK. Yes that 4 letter word no one wants to hear work. "We are saved unto good works". "He that keeps My works to the end.". "They were judged by their works". If you want clarity of scripture start by working for HIM. John 7:17 "He that DO the will shall know of the doctrine". God does not give these insights to be wasted but used. The lazy servant in Matt. 25 hid his talent. He was doing something all those years the King was gone. He was doing his thing and not the KINGS thing. Christians are doing for themselves today not God. Their focus is on many things but Christ and His work is not at the top of the list.

The seed that fell on GOOD ground says the first thing that man did was "He BEARED Fruit ". He knew exactly what was required & started work was immediately. When Jesus healed 10 lepers "HE said GO show yourselves to the priest and AS they WENT they were healed". Let us take the first step and show Him we are serious.

Personally I don't see how people fall for these fakes today. It is so obvious to me and some others. Even some I thought strong I found believing at least 1-2 of these fakes. Jesus church is a Spiritual body & church. Yes we go to any we want but we know what to accept and reject. We speak truth to anyone there who will listen. Sure we will be eventually be put out but we go to another. Or do like I had to after18 years. Start a study in your own home.

Be glad God didn't have a strike before now. Be glad He is sending the 2 Witnesses and 144,000 to warn Christians before this happens. That 144,000 will be joined by 200 million who will see the truth and come out these false churches and make Heaven. I pray you are one of them!!

CHAPTER 5
"Some Really Bad News"

R eal Christians will never say Bad news but just warnings for those not committed to giving our all for Jesus and Heaven. These bad news scriptures are very harsh but they're not going to happen to REAL Christians, only those lukewarm. Most all these scriptures come directly from Jesus Himself. Most like to think God is Love ONLY and don't want to hear the hard thing's He said. Like the seed on stony ground that fell away when persecution came because he was not told the hard parts that trouble would come. Paul said of the GOOD Christians even "…We are counted sheep for the slaughter". So if even the good accept our fate the lukewarm will not escape the worse fate that will come to them.

We are going to start with Hebrews 10:26-29 and as always I will write some of it but you should take time to read it all for yourself. "If we sin willfully after we have received the knowledge of the truth…" [Christians who fall away to sin]. "How much more of a SORER punishment [than Old Testament sinners] is thought worthy of them who trodden underfoot the SON of God". Those who turn back from Jesus salvation will be punished worse than a death and the unsaved. Verse 38 "If any fall back My soul shall have NO pleasure in him". So where is this forgiveness they keep saying we get? Verse 27 said there's "No more sacrifice for sins". And that is just for regular Christians. Pastors and leaders 1 Corin. 3:17 says "Him will God destroy" [going to the Lake of Fire]. 2nd Peter 2:21-22 says about the same thing in

"A dog returns to his vomit…better not to have known truth, than know it and fall away".

Isaiah 65:12-15 Jesus tells of those who didn't listen to His voice that "He would appoint them to the SWORD and they all will bow down to the SLAUGHTER". Jesus sentencing them to death, and hunger and thirst in the wrath of God Great Tribulation [hell on earth]. Some say this is not Jesus talking here? So let's look at Rev. 2:22-23 Jesus says in red those who follow Jezebel [the false prophet] "I will kill her children with DEATH." [Personally]. We need to stop thinking what Jesus should be and deal with Him by who He IS! He said "I and My Father are ONE". We can't play them against each other to avoid a whipping. He spit out Laodicea's Church and said "Who I love I rebuke and chasten". In Hebrews He says "If you endure chastening He will deal with us as SONS". Now maybe you can see the chastening is HELL, and dealing with them as SONS is at the 2nd Resurrection when they go to the New Earth; not Heaven.

Oh we have more bad news scriptures that most never considered. Revelation 7:9,14, 17 tells of the great number with white robes. Most all think these are in or going to heaven. WRONG! Re-examine this with me. Verse 14 John says he did not know who ALL these people were or where they came from. The angel had to tell him. "These are they who came out of great tribulation and washed their robes". Remember WHO Jesus said He would cast into Great Trib. In Rev. 2:22? Those who worship false teachings. Even "1 Strike"! Rev. 7:15 "..Worship in His Temple.." there is NO Temple in the Holy city so they cannot be in Heaven [Rev. 21:22 "I saw NO Temple there.". And verse 17 "God shall wipe all tears from their eyes…". This is written in Rev. 21:4 also. Going to Heaven is a joyful thing, so who are these crying their eyes out? The only people Jesus said several times would be crying; those He cast to "Outer darkness where there will be weeping and gnashing of teeth". Verse 16 gives even more proof they are not in Heaven. "They shall hunger and thirst No more". Remember Isaiah 65:12-15 the ones Jesus sent to the slaughter? He said they will HUNGER and THIRST. These are those same people. You see how the Bible connects the Old and New Testaments.

God can give you the ability to connect scripture like this IF you will do HIS work. Laborers are FEW remember. He says pray for workers. Do you have time and the boldness?

With just that many warnings to half stepping Christians I would be ready to get right NOW. But we have some more and harsher scriptures than those we just did. And I saved the most hidden one for last. By hidden I mean NO church elaborates on it. It's Revelation 3:10 "The Hour of Temptation". This is the church of Philadelphia and these are the people going to Heaven. This is the Little Flock who have endured to the end. They went through the 1st and start of the 2nd Beast and Devil. Jesus set before them and OPEN Door. I won't go into all the details of this or the other 7 churches now. You can see all the details of Revelation in my Revelation book "They Have Revelation Absolutely Wrong". But let's look at verse 9 here first; "I know the blasphemy of those who say they are Jews {Christians] but do LIE & are the church of satan…I will make them to come and worship at thy FEET & to KNOW that I have loved THEE" [not them the majority]. He adds the loved thee because the majority of Christians are in false teaching and think God on their side and not the side of the minority. I mentioned this earlier that when it comes to God the majority does not rule.

Now for the "Hour of Temptation". What is the temptation? When these leave in the Rapture and the majority are cast back it is the Great Tribulation wrath of God about to Happen on Earth. What will the temptation be? Most all Food and Water will be cut off from the whole planet. What little food and water is here the Beast will control. He will not give any to those cast back Christians UNLESS they get the 2nd and 3rd STRIKES of worshipping the Image and getting the Mark. That makes 3 strikes and Rev. 14:9-11 says even sinners who do all 3 are tormented forever! Yes they told us hell was forever but they were wrong. They say the Lake of Fire is really forever and that is wrong again. All come out of hell Rev. 20:12-15 at the 2nd Res. And those cast back Christians if they endured the Starvation and Thirst they can go to the New Earth and get their eternal life in a new body of flesh. No heaven for them period. So the Temptation is do we starve to death or not. If they want food and water the devil has it for them right there. Can you imagine that choice day after day?

They will all die anyway as will ALL not kept up in the Rapture. Rev. 14:17-18 shows another angel coming to send them back from the clouds they were raptured to. The 2nd Resurrection is called a Res. Because ALL are coming back from the DEAD. None survived. Jesus said in Matt. 24:22 "Except those days be shortened no flesh would survive…but for the Elects sake the days will be shortened". Shortened by the Rapture but all who weren't approved at the Judgment Seat of Christ and were cast down will die with the whole world Rev. 19:21.

I am not here to scare you. God gives us both sides of the coin to choose. He shows we can COME to Him because of His LOVE; or because we fear His PUNISHMENT. This is a no brainer for me. There is no way around HIS WORD. We can be forgiven for all our sins or pay for all of them.

The good news about those Christians cast back is after they've been to the clouds, and been rejected by Jesus in person that will give most of them the courage to except starvation and thirst unto death. Most will do anything to get their eternal life even if it is just on the New Earth. You see these cast back are the ONLY ones on earth who have a chance at eternal life still. All on earth who never accepted Christ have nothing to look forward to but the Lake of Fire and they know it. Once the world sees the Rapture they know God is real so there's no faith involved. We are saved by FAITH [believing without seeing the proof]. So now we know who the Tribulation saints are. They were not saved during the Great Trib. But were the ones cast back who accepted Jesus when faith was still involved. Those unsaved will also do you great harm because you have a chance and they don't.

Jesus said He will keep THESE from that time of horror. That's why this book. If you get even the 1st STRIKE you must go here!

CHAPTER 6
"Some Really Good News"

It's been said all my teachings are gloom and doom. But I often tell the great promises and mercy of God. He shows mercy even into the 1st Vail of WRATH He sends on the earth. How can any not see all these with the number one deed; "He so loved He sent His only Begotten Son". Not only that; "While we were YET Sinners He died for us". He didn't ask us to do anything first He reached out to us. Also He made it super easy because Jesus said; "As the serpent in the wilderness was lifted up, He also …". This means all they had to do was LOOK and live. Recognize the only way to LIVE was just LOOK. Looking means we KNOW that He is the ONLY way to Life. We are going to show many more great scriptures on the good news most never considered.

John 3:16 is the most famous scripture worldwide. I want to focus on the "Not PERISH" part; and farther down He says "Not CONDEMNED". Both these mean they won't go to the Lake of Fire. The Lake is forever gone never to return. That is perish and condemn. Hell is not the Lake. All come out of Hell at the 2nd Resurrection [Rev. 20:12-13] and some of those who did believed and accepted will go to the New Earth. But ALL the unsaved will go to the Lake. I won't elaborate on the details but they are in my Rev. Book. So to get in the safety zone of having a chance to live forever all we have to do is BELIEVE that he is the Son of God. That makes it so easy. After we believe Jesus starts speaking of doing MORE for the kingdom IF THEY WANT! He told the rich young ruler; "..If thou will be perfect". He doesn't have too; but if he does he can get HEAVEN. Just eternal life was mentioned before then for keeping the Law. Remember Jesus said in the parable on the Mount the Laws says; "But I say". The Law can't get us to Heaven, but to be HIS will. "Unless thy righteousness exceed theirs...you cannot enter into Heaven". If God had not put in place the 2nd chance for Christians very, very few would be saved. Always remember there will be a New Earth. Good News. No one seems to know who will be there.

Jesus warned about the numerous false Preachers coming in these last days that will be very convincing. But He gave a counter for them also in Matt. 24:14; "Before the end THIS Gospel of the kingdom will be Preached". So there will be no excuse of "I didn't know". He will make it absolutely clear what is truth and what is false. This will be the 144,000 and 2 Witnesses I keep speaking of. He is sending the 144,000 to counter the many demonic preachers and pastors who are as He said "Deceiving Many" [most]. He saw these days 2000 years ago and had a plan for us. In the book of Revelation He shows all the devils plans to us in advance. Satan can't sneak in anything on us. Good News!

Now many get frustrated about not being able to follow Gods word. Sin seems too powerful for us in this flesh. First we must know that no one could keep the Law, and Jesus seemed to add to it making it harder seemingly. But we have now the indwelling Spirit which they didn't have in the OLD Testament. Romans 6:14 "Sin shall NOT have dominance over us" [anymore]. I was redeemed from 24 years of IV drug use [junkie] and 31 years of Liquor. Plus other things in one day. It's the big 10 that we have power over ALL the time. Now all the ordinances He nailed to the Cross. Romans 14 tells us don't bother people about those little things anymore. We have freedom in Christ. "Happy is he who condemns not that thing he allows". Paul also says what to kick Christians out of the church for. God has a perfect for us and we have a perfect for us. God's perfect is not the same as ours. God just sees if we are fully committed in mind and heart. That is perfect enough for Him. With humans any mistake, we think makes us NOT good. Not with God.

"Who can lay any charge to God's elect"? Jesus is the one who says we are even charged. "Blessed is he whose sins are covered and not imputed". It doesn't say we didn't do wrong it says we will not be charged with it. Good News. And believe it not if we are "working for Him witnessing" those little things don't even come up. I say of a REAL Christian "Sin is the least of our worries". Real Christians aren't going to sin anyway. But IF we do "We have an advocate with the Father". Good News.

Remember Strike One you're out and the first strike is worship of the beast. And those get all 3 strikes forever burn in the Lake. God is so merciful even for those that when they get to the GREAT TRIB and the Wrath of God is poured out on earth the FIRST thing God does is send a noisome and grievous SORE on those that had the MARK. Why is this a good thing? Because the devil is still trying to get people on earth to get all 3 strikes because he knows they MUST be tormented with him and his angels forever. You see a FOREVER punishment was never meant for humans because we are weaker than angels. We will be punished for what sins we did. The more sins the more and longer punishment in the Lake of Fire; then the 2nd death for humans. Rev. 21:8 "..Shall have their PART in the Lake". So by sending the physical SORE, more human unsaved will stop before the 3rd strike and not get the Mark [Good News]. Yes the devil will kill them but would you want to walk around with a UGLY painful Sore that all could see? No, it will stop many from the real eternal torment. Now the words everlasting and not quenched Jesus uses in Mark 9 speaking HELL, not the Lake means: God is not sending ANY relief. And everlasting means as LONG as it LASTS! When all are dead in the Great Trib. Hell is over. Now the 2nd Res. And Lake of Fire come in. I hope you can understand that.

God said "I have no pleasure in the death of the wicked". Good News. "It is not His will that any should perish, but all come to repentance". Good News. He made us and a most beautiful planet for us to live on. Proof positive He loves us. Good News. When man first sinned in the Garden God set a plan in place to redeem us right away in Geneses 3:15 sending Christ. Good News. 1 Corin. 2:9

"Eye has not seen nor ear heard, neither has entered into the heart [mind] of man the things God has prepared for us". Good News. The best News of all to ME is we have a down payment already in the Comfort of the Holy Spirit. Philippian's 4:7 "Peace that passes all understanding" in our hearts [minds] all the time 24/7. GOOD NEWS.

Jesus said His "Yoke was easy". It's only hard when we try to play it both ways.

CHAPTER 7
"An Open Shame"

When Christians or anyone starts cutting corners on any job it gets to the point they don't know when or where to stop. When Christians decide there's some things they won't obey in the Bible they usually will add on more things to make life easier for themselves. When we decide there's even one thing in scripture we will not do, we may as well put the whole Bible down period. The Bible often speaks of "whole heart" and "forsake All". Little things lead to bigger things [sins]. Hebrews 6:6 speaks of Christians who fall away and it being impossible to renew them because "....They put Christ to an open shame". Hebrews 10:38 says "My soul shall have NO pleasure in him". "Salt that lost its savor is good for nothing but to be cast OUT". When we start cutting corners we are very likely to get the "1st Strike" and lose out on Heaven. Jesus is going to spit out the lukewarm and average Christian anyway. It is them who decided for one reason or another not to fully obey. The Jews hated the Samaritan's so strongly they wouldn't even hear of being nice to them. Racial hatred is just one thing some will not turn from. Money, sexual sins, pride, etc. are others people just will not change but try to justify it by the Bible.

Revelation 12:10 we see the devil in heaven because his 1,000 years is not quite up to return to earth. His 1st beast is on earth in charge doing his bidding; "The dragon gave him his power and his seat". He is telling God how horrible even His Christians are on earth and just let him have them ALL. "..He accuses them before

God night and day". And guess what? He is right. Jesus even said many will be deceived. While he is telling God this, in Rev. 13:8; "..All except those in the Lambs book are worshipping the 1ˢᵗ human beast getting the 1ˢᵗ strike. Even in the Old Testament God wouldn't destroy all the Jews because of the few good ones. God knows how to deliver the righteous and punish the bad. He has a day picked and will not be rushed. We want instant vengeance when we're wronged, but God "Inhabits eternity". Time is His. He can avenge us much better than we can avenge ourselves.

Let's look at this OPEN SHAME. God said in the Old Testament several times that His people give Him a bad Name to the Gentiles. Now in the New Testament we Christians are doing the same thing. Many will not even consider being saved after seeing us doing the same things they do and worse. They say Christianity doesn't work. In 2 Timothy 3:3 about Christians they are "Despisers of them that are good". Even in the churches! Imagine being put down for doing what Jesus says IN the Church? He said they will put Good Christians out the churches. Think of those who go back into deeper into sins and are seen by friends who knew they tried God? Now they're falling down drunk and doped up in a bar or whore house? Open Shame!! We make God look bad and WEAK. We are saying the devil is stronger than God. Why would anyone want to try our God?

Matthew 12:43-45 tells of an unclean spirit going out of a man [he gets saved] and the man doesn't do anything. He doesn't try to keep the spirit out by studying the Bible, going to church etc. So that spirit is wandering around looking for someone else to enter. He comes back across that same man and finds him EMPTY. He hasn't done anything to make himself strong. His mind is idle. So the demon says "..I will enter the house from whence I came....He goes in and last state of the man is worse than the first'. Paul tells us to put on the whole armor of God to be able to resist the devil. Christians in churches 20-40 years still don't know their Bible. The Sunday school classes are the same things they had for 30 years. The Preaching's are the same Bible stories with no new insights. Hebrews

5 Paul says "When we should be teachers we still have need to be taught the basics of Christianity. This is why most are afraid to discuss the Bible with the JHW on the street. They don't know their Bible. In 6-9 months they know more than most 40 year Christians. Shame! There are so many verses they have very wrong. And if you knew them they would never come to your house again, like they never come to mine.

We need to know the devil declares war on all who turn to Christ. We are born sinners belonging to the devil at death. He had us all in his back pocket until we accepted Jesus and His Power over the devil and his evil. So now is when we can see how the devil works as old temptations come upon us. Look who they come from? Friends, relatives, churchgoers. Now we see what Jesus meant "...A man's foes shall be they of his OWN household". When I quit drinking I found liquor everywhere and strangers gave me expensive liquors. I never drank it I sold it because it's not a sin to drink. Sin is to get drunk. But God wants ME never to drink. Watch how easy sex will come your way after you're saved. Proverbs says "...The adulterous woman will seek the Precious life". When you would screw anyone anytime they didn't want you. But when you got clean by Jesus you became precious. You have morals now. And the devil wants to bring down Jesus not just your little self. He's telling God "look how 2 faced they are". When a beautiful person offers you sex look harder. It's a demon behind that beauty. You will get your 1st strike when you compromise God's Laws.

Look at what God said about Job. Can God brag on you like He did Job? All who make Heaven will be like Job. All going to heaven will be fully committed to God like Him. About the 144,000; "They follow the Lamb Wherever He goes" [like Job]. Job lost everything and when the beast passes the "Can't buy or sell law we will lose everything also". Many say no one can be like Job. Oh yes we can and will and must! Heaven is for the ELECT. Jesus said it's EASY not hard, and His burden lite not heavy. All it takes is a one track mind. Decide you will not compromise God's word. Decide you will pray before you start doing your personal home studying. Yes home study. Revelation 3:20 God deals with individuals! "Behold I stand at the door and knock; if any man [singular] open the door, I will come in to him [singular] and sup with him [singular] and he [singular] with Me". 4 times He shows He wants deal with you alone. Every Christian has a personal relationship with Him. This is not a group plan.

Let's look at one more story of how serious the devil is about attacking Christians'. Scripture says "As a roaring lion he goes seeking who he may devour". And "he comes to steal kill and destroy". But look at what Jesus said he wanted to do to Peter His number one disciple. Luke 22:31 "Satan wishes to have you to sift you as wheat". To break him all the way down. To make a total fool of him to the world to embarrass Christ. Remember how foolish Sampson looked when they got him after cutting of his hair? They made a public spectacle of him. Satan wants to do this to all but especially leaders and Pastors. Pray for them hard! He wants to make God look bad, we are just the pawns.

Isaiah 5 God speaks of the Vineyard He built and did everything for it. Then it produced WILD [common grapes] Grapes. Just like the world. Just like the sinners. No difference. They talk the same. Steal, lie, fornicate the same. They compromise the same. They seek money the same. If we aren't different and stay different we will fall for the 1st Strike and Miss Heaven!

CHAPTER 8
"Is There an Easier Way"?

There has always been two ways to do things. The right way and the easy way. In Christianity so many get in then try to find a way around the so called hard parts. I say so called because none of it is really hard. When a person has their mind made up nothing is hard because they will just quickly find a way to the objective. If you have a winning ticket worth 50,000.00 and you have to get to a place to cash it within 4 hours you will find a way. If your car is broke you catch a bus, or call another ride. If the weather is bad it will not stop you. Your clothes will not stop you. Whatever it takes you will just do it. It will not seem hard, just and obstacle that must be gotten around. It's not hard it's necessary, period. If your winning ticket is only worth 10.00 then it may be too much trouble.

But we are looking at eternal LIFE in a place so beautiful human words cannot describe it. Jesus said of all humans John the Baptist was the greatest. But anyone that is in "The Kingdom of Heaven is greater than he". Being in Heaven is the most any being can ask for. Being there means can never ever die ever. You will be able to watch the universe and planets change. We won't have a 200lb body to lug around. God said "Eye has not seen nor ear heard what He has in store for us". And then if we look at the torment told us by the same person who told us of Heaven, we have a great choice to make. If we believe it and act we win BIG. If we don't believe and lose, we lose BIGGER. We cannot wish this choice away. It is the most important question every human born must answer. If we ignore the question we have made the choice already. "Except ye repent ye shall all likewise perish".

Most of my writings are for those who do believe but are just not understanding the importance of giving this your all. Most will half step this Christian life like Jesus said. They will be lukewarm. Not serious enough about Him or His work. He said every branch in Me that does not bear fruit His Father will TAKE it [him] away" [anyway]. So it's not just me saying this trying to put people down. Christians do more diligence to other things in their life than they do Him. These things Jesus said in Matthew 6 "Take no thought for our life what we shall eat, drink or wear". "The whole world seeks these things and God KNOWS we have need of these things". He says "Seek we first His Kingdom the ALL these will be added to us". It comes down to do we really believe Him? Do we really trust Him? "Without faith it is impossible to please Him".

What seems to make it hard to follow Christ? When we don't want to give up some things we love, so we look for a way around it and still be in good with God. I have seen it so many times and you have also. We each have something unique to us that another person isn't that into. Paul says "A sin that so easily besets US". Not someone else, but something that we particularly like. James says "When we are drawn away of our own lusts". So if I like liquor and want to keep getting drunk, I will either find a scripture that says I can keep doing it, or hope God forgives me for keeping on doing it? And Pastors will tell you "We all sin and no one's perfect". And that's all we need to keep it going. We are putting more faith in the Pastor than God's word. I'm just using drinking as an example because drinking is not a sin. Getting drunk is. I could use fornication, race hate, lying, stealing etc. but you get the point.

Sex is a powerful one people try to get around. God says "Marriage is honorable and bed undefiled". He knows we have a need for sex because He made us to produce. But He says ONLY if you're married period. Why would we try to get around that? It's simple if you want it do it His way. What about hate? The JEWS Hated the Samaritan's with a passion. If I hate someone, or a certain people or race for any

29

reason, is it so strong I will get my own self killed for that hate? "If we don't forgive neither will our Heavenly Father forgive us". No person is worth going to hell for. No person is cute enough to go to hell for, for sex. If we keep hell on our minds obeying Him would be much easier. When we start minimizing hell we get in trouble. Jesus said it's better to "Cut off our hands and feet, and pluck out our eyes than to go to hell". Do we really believe, period?

Let's look at the things Jesus said would make us think about falling away. First He says "The way is straight and narrow". No baggage can be brought in a narrow path. We can't go from side to side turning from left to right. He said all those on the broad path are going to hell, even though the sign says Heaven! Luke 6:22-23 He gets much harder with "Blessed are we when men hate us, put us away from them, and revile us.". Oh yes we will get terribly harassed by others. We will even get it from so called church folks. Remember it was the church folk who had Him killed. He said they will put us OUT the churches. He said "They will kill us and think they do God a service". But He said when it happens we are supper blessed and GREAT is our reward in Heaven. The more hate they show us the greater our payday will be. Isn't that worth whatever they do to us? Jesus said be like Him when they crucified Him. He had the power to kill them all or call "12 legions of angels" to defend Him. But He knew there's a day set for their Judgment and payback. They will cry like babies and run like chickens. He said "Fear not them that kill the [just] the body". Do we really believe? All who really believe will see it's worth it.

Just because our Pastors don't want to tell us the harsh parts of the Bible doesn't mean there's not going to be troubles. Jesus warned us many times if we care to read and check what the preachers say. The seed on stony ground fell away because he wasn't told the hard parts. Pastors don't want to lose members and money and chance running you away, so they tell you only the easy parts. Revelation 2:10 "Ye shall have tribulation 10 days". Churches say we will have no Tribulation. If people fall away the Bible says we will be "worse off than before". Pastors will not get away either. They get a worse punishment than you. Ezekiel 3:18-21 "If you fail to warn them their blood I will require at YOUR hand". "If you warn them you will have delivered your own soul". Pastors took a job so critical they should have double checked it first. James says "Be not many masters "teachers" for we shall receive the greater condemnation". No amount of money is worth what they get for misleading you and the members. 1 Corinthians 3:17 "If any man [leader] defile the temple [Member] him shall God destroy". I know what's at stake. It's not just you on the line, it's ME on the line also.

There is no easier way for me or you. Jesus said in John 12:48 "The words I speak the same shall judge you". We will be judged by the book not what the Pastors say or our opinions. Self-righteousness is when we decide what should get us into Heaven. When we decide what God should accept. I hear so many say God knows me and my heart. Yes He knows you are not doing what HE says.

Daniel 12:2 "Many that sleep in the graves shall arise at that time [1st Res.] some to everlasting life; some to SHAME and everlasting contempt". These are only Christians who are getting up here. Most of these Christians are getting their feelings hurt, like those who did "Wonderful works". "Great was the fall of that house" [person}. Imagine working 2 weeks and go to get your paycheck and there is none for you and it's your fault! We have all our breathing hours to double check what we are taught in church. I was raised in a denominational church also. But when I got grown I took a second look and saw they were off on several points that would keep me from Heaven. I was bold enough, and loved God enough to forget what they said and did to me and went with God and the truth, you can too.

Jesus said "My yoke is easy and burdens lite". It's not hard, it's easy. It's only hard when you try to have both ways. We can't have both. "What fellowship has light with darkness". If your joy comes from worldly people and things, you have a problem. "Love not the world, nor the thing's in the world". "He who hates his life in this world shall gain it unto eternal life". David said "His delight is in the Law of the Lord, and in that Law does he meditate day and night". I see so many friends and relatives trying to have both ways. That's the hard way. The EASIER way is to OBEY!

CHAPTER 9
"The 2 Main Traps"

J esus told the parable of Sower who went out to sow in Matthew 13. He showed 4 seeds 2 of which accepted Him then fell away. He is showing the 2 main reasons His followers will miss Heaven. The seed on stony ground and seed on thorny ground are the 2. The first was because of FEAR. The second because of material gain and other things they love or want more than Him. Later he will mention False Prophets as the main reason most fall. It's they who are letting the flock believe these falsehoods. Real leaders of Christ's church only tell the real truths no matter the consequences. And since He warns of the false coming in great numbers He is warning us in the Bible, if we care to double check our Pastors.

The seed on stony ground says "When persecution and tribulation come they fall away". But it says "they received the Word with JOY" [at first]. So most should wonder what went wrong. They were not told about the troubles to come. If they had been told about it they would have had the choice to not accept or prepare for the trouble. Remember Jesus said in Luke 14:28 to "Count the cost" before you join him. Jesus always told the whole truth. He wants all to know what they are getting into. He compared it to "Going up against and army that is double the size of yours". Showing it won't be that easy to win. Pastors want to fill their churches so they don't tell the hard parts.

It was the same in the Old Testament. God had to send outside Prophets to the people because the Priests wouldn't tell the people the truths. He warned of destruction of both Israel and Judah hundreds of years in advance. The false said "Peace, Peace". God said "There will be no Peace". One time 400 prophets went against just the one from God. And the Kings and people believed the 400. I said in Christianity the majority does NOT rule, or are right. Jesus said "Few find life". Yes even today people think because they are the majority in the churches they must be right. When Babylon attacked and destroyed the Temple they did not believe God would let anyone bother His Holy Temple. He did! In Samuel they took the Ark of the Covenant into a battle and God let that be captured also. They thought He wouldn't let anything happen because they were His chosen people. He did! Christians today are banking on Jesus mercy to forgive them for their disobedience. If He had not told us plainly in the Bible then we would have an argument. This laziness of not reading will not be an excuse.

Then the seed on thorny ground? "The cares of this world, and deceitfulness of riches choke the Word and he becomes UN fruitful". Does unfruitful send us to hell? Yes He is saying just that. Why will they be unfruitful? Because of other things in this world they want or love more than Him. Riches is the first thing mentioned. The love of money never seems to go away from us even when we are saved. It does right away to those of us who were dead serious from the start. Those the Father sent know it because the last seed that fell on good ground it says "They understood it and immediately bear fruit". So they knew exactly what was required. How? Because John 6 says "All that are taught of the Father come to Jesus". God put it in their Spirit at the start.

Back to the riches trap we know it seems all want more material things. It's because they still have and eye on the world, and its desire for the status money brings. Not the status Jesus brings. Money brings PRIDE the number 1 thing God Hates: Proverbs 6:17. Our pride cannot help but go up when we have extravagant things. New cars and clothes etc. bring a sense of pride to most. Of course we all must get new things at times. It's what's in our minds about these things that brings sin! Jesus gave many stories about riches and

FREDERICK SMITH

NONE of them were good. Check them. "A man's life consists not in the abundance of things he possesses". "What profit it a man to gain the whole world and lose his soul"? But it is still a great LURE to Christians, just like the UN saved. The devil tried to lure Jesus with the riches of the world and the power over it. He declined. A main fault is Christians do NOT trust God provide for them. So they stock up and stash money, JUST IN CASE! Jesus told us "Take no thought for your life, what you drink or wear". "For our Father knows we have need of these things".

The main thing about riches is it takes too much of our TIME. Time we could be using doing God's work. Not only are we showing a lack of Faith, but we are not Bearing Fruit! That is the wrong. Many try to have it both ways. They will try to get all the money they can, but only all the God they NEED to make it in. God will not be in competition with anything in our lives. Daniel 12:3 "They that turn MANY to righteousness shall shine as the brightness forever". John 15:8 Jesus said what makes the Father happy "That ye bear MUCH fruit". It's about the maximum, not the minimum! The lazy servant in Matthew 25 was doing something all the years the master was gone. He was doing and gaining for himself and not the Master. He hid the Masters work away. "All that is in the world, the lust of eyes; flesh; and pride of life is not of the Father but of the world".

Oh yes you will fall for the first strike because you want to get away from trouble with the beast. You will get the first strike so you can keep your material things. You won't be like Job who lost it all and still worshipped God. You will fall because you will WANT to believe that you don't have to lose it. The majority will be saying its ok, because we all are doing it in the churches. Unions can go on strike and get the boss to give in. But God will FIRE us ALL. Jesus said in John 6 to His 12 "Will ye also go away"? The whole crowd had walked away and left Him. He said in essence "You can go to".

1 Timothy 6 speaks on riches a lot saying anyone Preaching that GAIN is Godliness turn away". Today Christians flock to prosperity ministries in droves. Churches have become a fashion show, and the parking lots a car show. All Real Christians have what we NEED

34

and are not bothered by what the world says we need. The devil has many flashy things on TV every day that unsaved will strive for. Real Christians are not fazed by them. A car is just a car and shoes are just shoes. We are promised food; not steak and lobster. Jesus never owned anything His whole time down here. He knew all material things will perish. 2 Corinthians 4:18 "Things seen are temporary; things Unseen are eternal".

There are love songs about man's love for a woman. How he will give up comforts, and sleep in the rain etc. Give up all his money and swallow his pride. All for a human man or woman. Yet for an almighty God we skimp! It is He who has Life to give. It is He who has a Heaven for us. When we're about to die we all call on God. What are we saying about when things are good? When we are well? Psalms says "God will laugh at them" when they call while in trouble. Ezekiel 9:4-7 "He will not have pity nor will He spare any". "How can we escape if we neglect so great a Salvation".

Let's not think these things are too small for God to care about. He said He absolutely does care and will act on that. We have every warning to win Heaven. We know every trick of the devil to win Heaven. The only way we can lose is to NOT believe what He says. "The words I speak; the SAME shall judge you". Christians will fall for the first Strike if anything distracts them from Him being number one in their life. They will WANT to think something else, and not the truth of what He said. They will follow the majority. Be wise and start now to make Him number one.

CHAPTER 10
There's No Way Around This

All who call themselves Christians were supposed to have accepted the Bible as absolute authority. Jesus said "The scripture cannot be broken" and "The words I speak, the SAME shall judge you". I said before if we see anything in the Word we will not obey we may as well put down the whole book. We should know that most of the Bible are stories with examples for us. A small percentage is written in parables and mysterious signs like Revelation. Those need to be interpreted by someone who is truly lead by the Spirit. All others will MISS interpret it to their and YOUR destruction. 2 Peter 3:16 he says speaking of Pauls' writings on the last days "Hard to be understood & those unlearned & unstable [Taught by man's schools, not the Spirit] wrestle with [but teach anyway] to their own destruction". Peter and John were called UN learned and ignorant by the Pharisees in Acts because they hadn't went to their human schools. When in reality it was THEM who were really UN learned. Man's schools cannot teach God's mysteries! 7 times in Revelation Jesus said "He that has and ear let HIM hear what the Spirit SAYS to the churches". It's so sad that today's denominational churches require you have a degree from a human school to Pastor their churches. Paul was one of their best and highly trained graduates among the Pharisees. Jesus had to send him away 3 years to get all that junk out of him so He could put in him the real Spiritual truths. Galatians 1:10-18 tells the story. After he was saved he said "Immediately he conferred not with flesh and blood [humans] neither went to the Apostles". He didn't even check with Jesus chosen. And the greatest thing about this is after the 3 years alone being taught by the Spirit he did go to the 11 Apostles and talked. And it turns out exactly what Jesus had taught them, Paul had that SAME teaching!! How is that possible? It is with God. 1 John 2:27 "The anointing ye received teaches you all things, and need NOT any man teach you". Wow!

Jesus told the rich young ruler "Yet thou lack one thing; go sell all you have". Even one thing will keep you out of Heaven! Read that story again in Matthew 19. The rich man was trying to hide his wealth from Jesus. He wanted Jesus to say he was OK. He said "All the commands I have kept from my youth". He was expecting Jesus to ask that question about the 10 Commandments. He also had heard about Jesus teachings and knew Jesus NEVER said anything good about riches. So he came trying to trick Him into saying he was OK. Jesus told him about selling all he had. He had not fooled Jesus and neither can WE! Riches wasn't the problem, his faith IN his riches were! So many of us have things in our hearts [minds] we don't think even God can see. How wrong we are. If we are holding onto anything above Him He will see it. It will come out in the trial by Fire. 1 Corinthians 3:13 "The Fire shall test everyman's work". The beast's law of "Not buying or selling" will show if we love our material things and money more than Him. Jesus said "Where your treasure is there will your heart be also". If your treasure is on earth, so will your mind be. He said "Lay NOT up treasure on earth" period. Many will get the 1st Strike because of their earthly possessions.

So look at the absolute scriptures that there is NO way around, and my reason for writing this book. Revelation 15:2 specking of those ON the Sea of Glass who just went into Heaven after the Judgment Seat of Christ and were Not cast back like the Vine of the Earth in Rev 14:17-19. "They got victory over the beast; Image and Mark". All 3! Not trick of the devil did they fall for. Revelation 20:4 says the same "Did not worship beast; Image or get Mark". They passed all 3 tests also. So if they had fell for even ONE of the devil's tricks they would not be in Heaven.

If you can see I'm showing you the 1st strike comes a year or so BEFORE the other 2 strikes come. By then Christians WILL know that the beast is a devil and not a good guy. Rev 13:8 "All that dwell on earth shall worship the beast whose names are NOT written in the Lambs book of Life". All in the Lambs book go to Heaven. Rev 21:27 "None can enter into it but those whose names are written in the Lambs Book of Life. Rev 3:5 Jesus speaks of "Blotting names OUT of His Book". Just like our names went IN the book, they can come OUT His Book! Now if all these are in Heaven WHO will be on the New Earth? Now you're thinking. Some people must be on it, but who and why? Most of those who MISSED Heaven were cast back will have another chance at the 2nd resurrection. Rev 20:11-15 the Book of Life is opened again. But it's not Jesus book, it's the Fathers book. Jesus has already taken His out at the 1st time and they were married to Him in 19:7-9. If they kept Gods laws even though they were rejected and cast back, they can get the New Earth. Rev 7:14, 17 & 12:17.

Matthew 7:27 "Great was the fall of that house" [person & they were devastated]. I can feel the hurt and grief of these people and do NOT want this to happen to any of you. This is why I'm writing. They will still be on the earth when they see their mistake. If the devil came with the MARK first, people would know not to do that and who he really is. But being slick he comes with just THINKING he is a great guy. Because he knows God will not accept you into Heaven if you fall for that. When they realize they have messed up they won't get the Mark or worship the Image but it's too late for Heaven. Please do like I'm doing and think of the way these fooled Christians will FEEL at this time. Feel it! Paul said we "Weep and rejoice when our brothers weep and rejoice". We hurt when they hurt. I hurt NOW just thinking of these people. Jesus felt it and described it "Weeping and Gnashing of teeth". Weeping because they got their feelings hurt. Grinding teeth for the pain their going through.

As I said at the start it's not because they believe the beast 100%, but because they HATE the message the 2 Witnesses bring them from GOD. Remember they want an easier way. They don't want to forsake all. They don't want to love everybody. Especially of every RACE! They don't want to have marry to have sex. They do love their families MORE than God. They want to go from luxury down here, to luxury up there. They want the Pastor to do their studying. They want the others to do their witnessing. They want to get Raptured out of here before any trouble starts, & that's exactly what their Pastors tell them. Wow! "I am the Lord thy God; I change NOT". Do we actually think we can change His rules and His mind? When we stop thinking that this journey becomes EASY.

If churches taught this I would not have had to write this. You must be the judge by checking the scriptures. Your Pastors have reason to be bias on their answers to you about this. They want their church seats filled. They won't be filled with harsh sermons like the scriptures in this book. Revelation was written in a mystery because it was not to be revealed until THIS time. Now God is ready to show all who will DO the work the insights. John 7:17 "He that will DO the will shall know of the doctrine". And Jesus said "Pray the Lord of the harvest send LABORERS". With workers so badly needed why would He not accept many more people? He will "IF" they are dead serious. Of that 144,000 He has already going to Heaven and helping the 2 Witnesses that 144,000 will turn into 200,000,000. Yes that's how many of you will come out of false teaching and make Heaven also. That's good news. So be one and not get that 1st Strike with us

CHAPTER 11
"Meat in Due Season"

Jesus said this in Matthew 24:45 at the end of telling about the Last Days. He said WHO will be worthy for Him to give the Knowledge of the End Times to Preach? Meat in due season means the right teaching at the right time. What things? The things that will be happening at the end. Revelation! This information was not given back then. John saw the whole vision and he will be one of the 2 Witnesses to preach it. Yes he's coming back. But there needs too be many more teaching these things because there about 2 billion who profess Jesus [Christians]. You can be one of the helpers. The 144,000 are just to help get it started. There are great rewards still to be had. All the heroes of Bible are not just in Hebrews 11. We are still in a fight.

I repeat the scripture of John 7:17 "He that will DO the will of the Father SHALL know of the doctrine". He will enable you to understand what the mysteries are NOW. It was saved for this time, and that time is NOW. If the churches through the ages had known the meanings they would have been obsessed with our time, and not the work of saving souls in their own time. Jesus had to open the minds of the 11 apostles in Luke 24:45 for them to understand. Even after 3 years with Him and hearing, they did not understand. He would ask them at times if they understood, and they lied and said they did, but they didn't. So don't feel bad about not seeing these things. Remember laborers are greatly needed so ask for this job. Just know all hell will come at you. Are you ready for that? Jesus said "The gates of hell shall NOT prevail against [us] it".

I tell my class they only need me [or any preacher} till they learn to follow the leading of the Holy Spirit themselves. Then they don't need me anymore and can go out on their own. I'm here if they do need something. Most Pastors don't want their members to ever leave them and start a ministry. The more qualified to start another a ministry, the more the Word of Christ will reach.

Just remember our place and stay humble. Pride is the number one thing God hates. Don't let money get to you. Many Pastors got corrupted by the money. They didn't know how much money would come in and got money fever. I do like Paul did in 1 Corinthians 9. He said he will not take money for preaching even though he could. So no one could bring that against him. I don't take offerings because God provides for my needs without offerings. I don't seek material expensive things and neither does any REAL Preacher for Christ. But if you need it take.

Remember those are not your people but Christs'. Pastors have tendency to think they own people. They want to keep that money and offering forever. Don't expect to have a LARGE crowd. If you are teaching both the HARD and the easy many will leave because of the hard things. Timothy says "They will heap to themselves teachers having itchy ears". Pastors will only tell what they want to hear. Acts 20:30 Paul says "They will draw away people after them" [selves].

Never get envious of big churches, or their big money. You work for Christ and our payday is yet to come. We are still on a JOB. Any not preaching for Christ and the hard truths, are preaching for the devil period. If they think so or not! Warn them what's to come, because very few will!

SUMMARY

J esus said "What I tell you in the ear that shout ye from the rooftops". Yes He deals with individuals. But many say God said this or that to me. What he says He ALSO said in the Bible. If it's not in the Bible He did NOT tell them anything. People murder and say God said to do it. All of these seemingly new things you're hearing, you'll SEE they are in this same Bible that's been around for years. All churches and pastors have these in their Bibles. Look at their interpretations of these Rev scriptures then look at mine. I gladly tell you their side but they don't want you know any side but theirs. Why?

Time is too short to take chances. Be thankful God let you live this long to double check what you have believed will get you into Heaven. I said we are in the 6th trumpet already. It's coming to a close quick. "Behold I come quickly". We can tell by the pollution of the planet and global warming that this planet cannot last much longer.

However misses this first trick of the devil and gets their 1st strike, absolutely will not go to the Heaven they had their hopes on. Heaven is there and Jesus ONLY Preached Heaven not the New Earth. Why? Because He wanted us all to make Heaven. Why preach 2nd place when we can be 1st? And once the 1st Resurrection and His Judgment Seat is over Jesus is DONE with humans. He has HIS. Yes he will rule over those on the New Earth, but His job was to get a people for Himself. And we can be one.

Isaiah 56:10-12 speaks of false leaders. It calls them "Greedy; dumb dogs; cannot bark [to warn]". Any Pastor or church that does not tell you what coming is in big trouble with God. Even worse they will tell lies or guesses about the End times rather than say they don't know. God saw these fakes and said MANY would come and deceive MOST of you. When will you check? The whole mystery book called Revelation tells us all the devils tricks he is going to bring on us. We can beat him with this information. Just One wrong move and we miss Heaven. Why? Because Jesus serious followers won't fall for any of it. They are not better than anyone else. They just put in the work and did the studying.

2 Thess. 2:10-12 is one of the harshest scriptures you or I have ever read. It says "For this cause GOD will send them strong delusion that they should believe the LIE; that they all might be DAMNED". Wow! God doing this! Because they "Believed & Received not the truth". Meaning something has PASSED. What passed was they did not believe His 2 Witnesses and 144,000 when they had the chance. They had just been killed by the 1st beast at this time. Is this getting serious to you yet?

I said a lot about Denominations in this book. So let me explain it more. We are to go to church period. It's what we know in our hearts that counts. All denominations have some false teaching in it. Some false teachings will not send us to hell like Paul says in Romans 14. While we are there we speak the truths of the Bible to anyone who asks. We don't go around trying to disrupt the service. But if they ask!! Some Pastors and people will get super angry and put you out after a while. That's ok, Jesus said they will do that. He says just go to another city [church]. We must stand up for the truth because the truth is standing up for Jesus Himself. "He who denies Me and My words; I will deny before My Father". When your knowledge gets to the teaching level you can start your on studies in your homes. But WAIT till the Spirit gives you the go ahead like He did me. By taking the abuse and rejection in the Churches you are being made stronger for when the really hard times come.

God is just as sure in His WRATH as He is
His Mercy. I'm praying hard for you.
Bro. Fred

Printed in the United States
by Baker & Taylor Publisher Services